THE BURNING OF COLUMBIA, S.C.

THE BURNING OF COLUMBIA, S.C.:

A REVIEW OF NORTHERN ASSERTIONS AND SOUTHERN FACTS

By
Daniel H. Trezevant

A new edition edited by
Karen Stokes

SHOTWELL
COLUMBIA · SO. CAR.
EST. 2015
PUBLISHING

The Burning of Columbia, S.C.: A Review of Northern Assertions and Southern Facts

Copyright© 2022 by Karen Stokes

Produced in the Republic of South Carolina by

SHOTWELL PUBLISHING LLC

Post Office Box 2592

Columbia, So. Carolina 29202

www.ShotwellPublishing.com

Cover Image: Historic American Buildings Survey, Creator. Millwood Ruins, U.S. Route 76 Garners Ferry Road, Columbia, Richland County, SC. South Carolina Richland County Columbia, 1933. Documentation Compiled After. Photograph. https://www.loc.gov/item/sc0096/.

ISBN: 978-1-947660-76-2

FIRST EDITION

10 9 8 7 6 5 4 3 2 1

Contents

INTRODUCTION

The Burning of Columbia, S.C.: A Review of Northern Assertions and Southern Facts was published as a pamphlet in 1866. The author, Dr. Daniel H. Trezevant, was a resident of Columbia, a physician, and an eyewitness to the city's occupation, sacking, and destruction by the army of General William T. Sherman on February 17th, 1865. Dr. Trezevant first authored a series of newspaper articles that appeared in the *Daily South Carolinian*, and these were then collected and published as a pamphlet with a preface written by Felix G. De Fontaine, the newspaper's editor. In the 1950s, a facsimile edition of the pamphlet was reprinted which included a foreword by South Carolina historian A. S. Salley, and this is the version presented here.

Both Salley and De Fontaine included some biographical information about Dr. Trezevant in their prefatory remarks, to which may be added the following comments by John T. Trezevant, who compiled a family history published in 1914:

> Dr. Daniel Heyward Trezevant, when the writer knew him from 1864 to 1867, was one of the most magnificent specimens imaginable of a dignified, accomplished physician. He was the friend and intimate of all the leading families in Columbia, in which city no man stood higher. He lost one son in the Mexican war, two were killed in the Confederate war, and when Columbia was burned his house was fired by drunken Federal soldiers while he stood by and looked on appealingly, in vain, for the privilege of carrying from the burning building the pictures of those who were dear to him, and who had died years before. All during the hard times of the last year of the war, the old gentleman had his house full, not only of his own children, but grandchildren, and no

man in Columbia gave more liberally to charity and to the aid of the many who saw starvation coming in the door during that trying period.

In the fateful month of February 1865, one of Dr. Trezevant's patients was Mrs. Eliza Haskell Lee, a refugee from Charleston whose health was precarious. She was recovering from an illness and due to give birth to a child very soon. When Sherman's forces first entered the city on February 17th, Dr. Trezevant petitioned one of the officers, Col. George Stone, to place a guard to protect Mrs. Lee and her house, but his request was refused. She went into labor that very night and gave birth to a daughter, Katie. Throughout the evening, while Dr. Trezevant was present to attend to the lady, groups of Sherman's soldiers came in, ransacking the house, destroying food supplies, and even setting fires. Mrs. Lee recalled in her memoir:

> Our house was filled with soldiers drunken and sober; and three of the drunken ones had been turned from my door, by our kind old doctor. But when my infant was but an hour old, another party, with segars in their mouths, fortunately sober, burst into the room. My sister, the only other occupant of the room, sprang from her seat, with my baby on one arm, and the other outstretched in agonized entreaty, "For God's sake leave the room; my sister is very ill, and you will kill her!"[1]

The story of the soldiers who first tried to intrude on Mrs. Lee while she was giving birth was also recorded in the diary of Grace Brown Elmore, a Columbia resident who wrote that the soldiers, jeering that they wanted to "see a dam rebel born," were prevented from entering Mrs. Lee's bedroom by Dr. Trezevant, who braced himself against the door and declared, "You'll enter only over my body."

In the manuscript collections of the South Caroliniana Library there is a bound volume dated "1865" in which Dr. Trezevant recorded many of his thoughts and observations about the burning

---

1   Lee, "Reminiscences."

of Columbia. Much of it seems to the basis of his newspaper articles and the pamphlet that followed. The manuscript journal also contains copies of correspondence, including a copy of a letter that the doctor wrote to his brother Theodore in England in August 1865, in which the doctor lamented that "in the conflagration of Columbia, I lost everything I had in the world."[2]

In the pamphlet, Dr. Trezevant scornfully quotes from a memoir written by Major George Ward Nichols of the United States Army, in which the officer claimed that he had no knowledge of any "outrages" committed by the soldiers in his army against women or children. Trezevant's own experience with Mrs. Lee, as well as many other incidents about which he learned from fellow Columbians, were ample proof that Nichols' claim was absurd.

The 1865 manuscript journal kept by Dr. Trezevant contains accounts and details of certain incidents that were not included in his published pamphlet. In particular, those details dealing with outrages against women (which a Victorian gentleman would be disinclined to publicize) were omitted from the published account. The manuscript journal also includes some of the female victims' names. In one passage, he mentions Mrs. T. B. Clarkson, who stated that "They [Sherman's soldiers] threw fire balls among the women and girls who had sought shelter in the park."

This detail about the women and girls in Sidney Park is corroborated in a letter written by Mrs. Elizabeth May Evans Axson (1828-1901), who was in Columbia at the time of its occupation and burning. She wrote to her aunt in June 1865: "Many took refuge in the beautiful Park. It was filled with women and children. But firebrands, turpentine balls, torpedoes and every kind of combustible was set on fire and thrown on them." Another Columbia resident, Miss Louisa R.

---

2   The correspondence in the journal dates from 1865 to 1866 and consists of copies of official military correspondence as well as Trezevant's letters to his brother in England and Fraser, Trenholm & Company. These chiefly pertain to conditions in South Carolina in the months following the end of the war, the freedmen, his parents' estate, and business and financial matters.

McCord, reported in a letter of March 1865: "Crowds of women and children gathered in the park and Yankees actually stood on the hill above and threw the hand grenades among them."[3]

The manuscript journal also includes the following passages:

> An officer whose kindness to some ladies had induced them to keep to and converse with him, upon being questioned whether Sherman mean to burn the town, replied that he could not say as he did not know but he hoped not. It was now 9 o'clock at night as he paced the garden, he stopped near the gate and said to the ladies in the piazza, ah ladies I regret to see it, there goes the signal, as some rockets ascended. Your beautiful city is doomed. Instantaneously as it were a number of fires were seen breaking from different quarters of the city.

> No woman nor child was injured or insulted—this is a boast of Nichols and so far as the Carolina lady was concerned I think that there were but few exceptions. The Yankees gallantry, brutality and debauchery was confined to the negro. He associated with them ... It was not at all unusual to see a Yankee soldier with his arms around a negro woman even in the common thoroughfares, hugging and kissing a mulatto girl when he could find one so degraded ... It was of hourly occurrence ...

> The case of Mr. Shand's old negro woman who after being subjected to the most brutal indignities from seven of the Yankees was, at the proposition of one of them to finish the old bitch, put into the ditch and her head held under the water until life was extinct. Yet with such facts known to Nichols and the officers of the army, he throws out the boast that no woman or child had been injured.

---

3   Stokes, *South Carolina Civilians*, 56.

Mrs. T. B. Clarkson was seized by one of the soldiers or officers and dragged by the hair and forced to the floor for the purpose of sensual enjoyment. She resisted as far as practicable, held up her young infant as a plea for their sparing her and succeeded, but they took her maid and in her presence threw her on the floor and had connection with her. Mrs. G.[4] told me that Mrs. C[larkson] informed her of the fact.[5]

To take a lady by the hair of her head and drag her to the ground for the purpose of pollution is somewhat like an outrage and when she held her infant up and entreated for the sake of the child, then to seize upon her maid and make her the substitute in the presence of her mistress, out Herods Herod and would make even Beast Butler ashamed.[6] Yet this thing was perpetrated by Yankees.

They pinioned Mrs. McCord and robbed her.[7]

They dragged Mrs. Gwynn by hair of her head about the house. Mrs. G. told me of a young child of about 16, Miss Kinsler, who they (three officers) brutally ravished and who became crazy from it. She saw the young lady and knew her.

---

4   After the "G" the rest of the lady's name is added in darker writing as "Guerard." There are two initials before "Mrs. Guerard" that are difficult to interpret with certainty.

5   This was Septima Louisa Screven Clarkson (1835-1911) , the wife of Rev. Thomas Boston Clarkson, Jr. (1833-1889). Her daughter Julia, who had been born in June 1864, was probably the infant mentioned in Trezevant's account.

6   "Beast Butler" was Union General Benjamin Franklin Butler (1818-93). On May 15, 1862, he issued an order to his occupying army in New Orleans to treat any Confederate woman who showed them disrespect as "a woman of the town plying her avocation."

7   Mrs. Louisa S. McCord (1810-1879) was a noted author who, during the war, devoted herself to the care of wounded Confederate soldiers in Columbia. Gen. Sherman's second in command, Gen. Oliver O. Howard, used her house as his headquarters when the city was occupied. Before he arrived, Union soldiers were pillaging her house, and one of them seized Mrs. McCord by the throat and tore a watch off her dress.

In a journal of 1865, James J. McCarter, a Columbia alderman, also reported evidences of outrages against women—both black and white—by Sherman's soldiers, writing: "The bodies of several females were found in the morning of Saturday stripped naked and with only such marks of violence upon them as would indicate the most detestable of crimes ... the town seemed abandoned to the unrestrained license of the half drunken soldiery to gratify their base passions on the unprotected females of both colors."[8]

Dr. Trezevant's pamphlet presents proofs that it was Sherman's army which bore the responsibility for burning Columbia, despite the general's attempts to place the blame elsewhere (mainly on a Confederate commander, General Wade Hampton). The doctor also emphasizes the overwhelming advantage in numbers that the northern army had over the much smaller number of Confederate defenders in the area, which consisted of a few thousand troops under the command of generals Wade Hampton, M. C. Butler, and Joseph Wheeler (all of whom were subordinate to General P. G. T. Beauregard, the commander in Charleston).

Trezevant devotes much attention to one of Sherman's officers, the aforementioned Major George Ward Nichols, and excoriates him for some of the outrageous, false, and boastful claims he made in his memoir, *The Story of the Great March,* which was published in 1865.[9]

---

8   James J. McCarter's "Journal" is found in the Library of Congress, Manuscripts Division.

9   Other writings by Nichols are equally dubious. In 1866, he published an article in *Harper's New Monthly Magazine* in which he described a conversation he had in Columbia with a Mr. Huger, "a well known citizen of South Carolina." Nichols claimed that Huger had confirmed to him that it was Confederate troops who were responsible for most of the pillaging in Columbia. This "well known citizen" was Mr. Alfred Huger (1788-1872), the postmaster of Charleston, who was in Columbia with his family in February 1865. When Mr. Huger learned of Nichols' article, he wrote a response to the editor of the *New York World,* denying, among other things, that the conversation reported by Nichols ever took place. In 1867, Nichols published an article in *Harper's* about Wild Bill Hickok. The story made Hickok famous but was widely criticized for false and exaggerated accounts of the exploits of this Old West folk hero.

To give one example, Trezevant comments on Nichols' indignation that some of Sherman's foragers, or "bummers," had been killed while they roamed the countryside after the burning of Columbia:

> There are several other remarks of Nichols' that ought to be noticed. Several soldiers were found on the road-side, who had been killed, either by the citizens or by Confederate soldiers. They belonged to a gang who had been firing and pillaging the country in every direction, and simply met the fate they deserved. The virtuous indignation of the General is aroused and Sherman gave Kilpatrick orders to hang and shoot prisoners who fall into his hands, to any extent he considers necessary. Nichols' fire on the occasion, calls out: "Shame on Beauregard and Hampton and Butler," and asks, "Has the blood of their fathers become so corrupted, that the sons are cowardly assassins. If this murderous game is continued by their friends, they will bitterly rue the day it was begun." Without knowing why or wherefore those men were punished, an order is given for the hanging of the prisoners, though Sherman, when alluding the circumstance, acknowledges that his foragers committed many acts of atrocity.

General Sherman and General Hampton exchanged correspondence about the killing of these foragers. Walter Brian Cisco wrote of this in his biography of Hampton:

> As he moved through the South Carolina upcountry, Sherman was informed that two parties of foragers near Feasterville in Fairfield District had been captured and killed. They were found with a sign proclaiming "Death to all foragers." Sherman penned a letter to Hampton on February 24, asserting his right to collect provisions "directly of the people." He had "no doubt this is the occasion of much misbehavior on the part of our men," but threatened to begin killing Southern

prisoners if it happened again. Sherman prepared to execute eighteen Confederates held at the Lancaster Courthouse. Hampton fired back a reply. He denied issuing any orders to kill foragers after capture, but emphasized that every man had the right to defend his home and family, "and from my heart I wish that every old man and boy in my country who can fire a gun would shoot down, as he would a wild beast, the men who are desolating their land, burning their homes, and insulting their women."[10]

Mary Chesnut's famous diary reports an incident of the "misbehavior" of some of Sherman's soldiers—in fact a horrible incident of rape and murder—which was related to her by her husband, General James Chesnut:

> I asked him what that correspondence between Sherman and Hampton meant. This was while I was preparing something for our dinner, and his back was still turned as he gazed out of the window. He spoke in the low and steady monotone that characterized our conversation the whole day, and yet there was something in his voice that thrilled me. "The second day after our march from Columbia, we passed the M------'s. He was a bonded man, and not at home. His wife said at first that she could not find forage for our horses. Afterwards she succeeded in procuring some for us. I noticed a very handsome girl who stood beside her as she spoke to me. I suggested to her the mother the propriety of sending her daughter out of the track of both armies; there was so much straggling, so many camp followers, and no discipline on the outskirts of the army. The girl answered quickly: 'I will stay with my mother.' That very night, a party of Wheeler's men came to our camp. They had passed the house later and found horror and destruction, the

---

10   Cisco, *Wade Hampton,* 156-57.

mother raving of what had been done. This outrage was done before her very face, she being secured first. This straggling party of the enemy, after their crime, moved on. There were seven of them, and the woman said they had been gone but a short time. Wheeler's men went off in pursuit at full speed, overtook them, cut their throats, and marked upon their breasts: 'These were the seven.'" "But the girl?" I whispered. "Oh, she was dead."[11]

In his book *The Uncivil War*, Thomas Bland Keys compiled hundreds of reports of war crimes and atrocities committed by the Union Army that appear in that army's own official records. Those reports, along with Southern sources like Dr. Trezevant's book, and countless letters, diaries, and other primary sources of the 1860s, reveal the brutality of the war that was waged against the South. Dr. Trezevant considered it vitally important to document the brutality that occurred in his city and state so that it would not be disputed or forgotten, and Thomas Bland Keys compiled his own book for the same reason, concluding his introduction with this statement: "What hundreds of thousands of lawless men did to the South should never be forgotten. Descendants of those men should be cognizant of their lineage."

---

11 Chesnut, *A Diary from Dixie,* 496.

THE BURNING OF COLUMBIA, S.C.:

A REVIEW OF NORTHERN ASSERTIONS AND SOUTHERN FACTS

Daniel Heyward Trezevant, the author of the following pamphlet, was born in Charleston, South Carolina, March 18, 1796. He was of the fifth generation descended from Daniel Trezevant, one of the Huguenots who fled from France upon the revocation of the Edict of Nantes.

His father was Peter Trezevant and his mother was Elizabeth Willoughby Farquhar, only child of Robert Farquhar, a merchant of Charleston. Farquhar was a native of Bilbo, Scotland, who left Scotland about 1770 for South Carolina. At the same time his brother, John Farquhar, went to India as a cadet in the Bombay establishment. John Farquhar had engaged in chemical experiments in his lei sure hours and had thereby acquired a practical knowledge of chemistry. The gunpowder manufactured at Pultah having been found unsatisfactory, Farquhar was selected by General Cornwallis, then governor-general of Bengal, to enquire into the matter and render his assistance. This proved sore valuable that he was made superintendent of the factory, and ultimately became sole contractor to the government.

When, after reaching middle life, he returned to England he was worth about a half a million sterling. He became a partner in the agency of Basset, Farquhar & Co. in London, and purchased a share in the famous brewery of Whitbread. His wealth, as it accumulated, was devoted to the purchase of estates and investment in the funds.

John Farquhar died suddenly, July 6, 1826, and his estate, amounting to about a million and a half pounds, was divided among seven nephews and nieces. One of the latter was Mrs. Peter Trezevant, as heretofore related. When the news arrived of his wife's good fortune Peter was a bank clerk in Charleston. He is said to have remarked that he had been poor all of his life, but that thereafter he expected to live on turbot, and it is also said the Charlestonians who afterwards dined with him in England found him living up to expectations.

The couple had thirteen children of whom Daniel Heyward was the fourth. He graduated at the South Carolina College in 1813; attended a medical college and began the practice of medicine in Columbia before the good fortune befell his parents.

Dr. Trezevant was married in St. Michael's Church, Charleston, May 3, 1820, to Ann Sewall, of New York, by whom he had eight children, the fourth of whom was named Daniel Heyward, born July 10, 1829. He enlisted in the Palmetto Regiment in the War with Mexico, and was killed at Chepultepec.

Mrs. Trezevant died August 20, 1838, and the Doctor married next, November 15, 1841, Epps Goodwyn Howell, by whom there were six more children.

Dr. Trezevant died in 1873.

By A. S. Salley

PREFACE

Much discussion has been evoked on the question as to who is responsible for the burning of Columbia, and the outrages connected with that event. In South Carolina, the author of the crime is known to be Gen. WILLIAM T. SHERMAN; but among communities outside of the State, who have not been made familiar with the facts, ignorance on the subject naturally enough prevails. At the North especially, where the press has chosen to circulate only the one sided statements of its contributors, the public effect to believe that Columbia was destroyed by the Confederate authorities; and books have been written, in which falsehoods are gravely promulgated to establish this theory. The object of the present review is to put all doubts on the subject at rest forever.

The writer of the following pages is one of the most highly respected citizens of South Carolina, and has been a resident of Columbia for more than fifty years. He was present during the most trying scenes of the conflagration, a personal witness of many of the outrages narrated, and as the reader will discover, is in every way competent to handle his subject with a clearness and force which its importance demands.

The articles were originally published in the *Daily South Carolinian* at the request of many citizens have been embodied in a more permanent shape.

F. G. DEFONTAINE,

Editor Daily South Carolinian

THE BURNING OF COLUMBIA

"Who is to blame for the burning of Columbia is a subject that will long be disputed." So writes Conyngham in his history of Sherman's grand march, but I think he solved the difficulty by his acknowledgments before he threw out his question and doubt.[12] That controversy can be easily settled whenever the specifications on which the charge is made, are brought to issue; after issue, the truth will be known. It is very evident that the belief of the writer was fairly made up; than on his mind, there was little doubt as to who was the cause of the destruction of the city, and that Sherman was the man. In discussing the question, he, by implication, charges Gov. Magrath and Gen. Hampton with being partly to blame; but as the statement which he makes, is founded on an erroneous impression, with the correction of that error it must fall.

In the preceding part of his book there are several circumstances stated which are necessary to be brought into consideration before we follow him in his accusation; and it will be found by his acknowledgement, and that of others, that the city was in the hands of the Yankee army some time before the fire commenced; that they got quiet possession, it having been turned over to them by the Mayor, and that all matters under the command of Colonel Stone were peaceably and properly arranged. There is no mention of any insubordination, and not a hint of a fire existing in the city. Under these circumstances, Stone held the city for about one hour before the appearance of Sherman; and Mayor Goodwyn[13] and Aldermen Stork and McKenzie, certify that when they passed the cotton with

---

12   David P. Conyngham (1825-1883), a war correspondent for the *New York Herald,* accompanied Sherman's army on its campaigns in Georgia and South Carolina. In 1865, his history of these campaigns was published as *Sherman's March Through the South.*

13   Dr. Thomas Jefferson Goodwyn (1800-1878), a physician, was elected mayor of Columbia in 1863.

Colonel Stone, it was not on fire, nor did it take fire for some time after the authority was vested in him. The Mayor also says: "Gen. Sherman sent for me the morning after the city was burnt, and said that he regretted very much that it was burnt; that it was my fault, in suffering liquor to remain in the city, when it was evacuated." The evidence of other gentlemen will be brought to bear upon the time when, and the manner how it did take fire, for they saw the whole affair. Let me now return to Conyngham's remarks, and it will be seen that as far as possible he corroborates the statement I have just made: "Our march through the city was so orderly that even the Southerners began to bless their stars that the reign of terror was over, and that a reign of peace and security, like that at Savannah was about being inaugurated." "I spent the evening in the Capitol, looking over the archives and libraries. Part of Col. Stone's brigade—I think the 13th Ohio, Col. Kennedy's regiment—was on duty there. Towards night, crowds of our escaped prisoners, soldiers and negroes, intoxicated with their new-born liberty, which they looked upon as a license to do as they pleased, were parading the streets in groups." No mention as yet of any fires about the town, or of any cotton having been found flying about, or on fire, but he writes: "As soon as night set in, there ensued a sad scene indeed." (This is the time Sherman reports that the fires were in full blast, and that he had called in the rest of Gen. Wood's division.) "The suburbs were first set on fire"—by whom? the prisoners and soldiers and negroes for it was not within 500 yards of the cotton that Sherman saw burning, "*some assert*, by the burning cotton which the rebels had piled along the streets. Pillaging gangs soon fired the heart of the town, then entered the houses, in many instances, carrying off articles of value. The flames soon burst out in all parts of the town," &c., &c." "I trust I shall never witness such a scene again—drunken soldiers rushing from house, emptying them of their valuables, and then firing them; negroes carrying off piles of booty, and grinning at the good chance and exulting like so many demons; officers and men revelling on the wines and liquors until the burning houses buried them in their drunken orgies. I think this looks very much like a city turned over to the soldiery to do with as they please; corresponds with what they said—that were authorized first to sack, and then to burn it—that they, both officers and men, had so determined, and that it met with Old Bill's full approbation. "The frequent shots on every side told that some victim had fallen—shrieks and groans and cries of distress resounded from every side. A troop of cavalry—I think the 29th Missouri—were left to patrol the streets; but I did not once see them interfering with the groups and pillage the houses." Methinks after penning such a description, that there was no occasion to ask "who was to blame for the burning of Columbia." But let us see what more he has to report: "True, Gens. Sherman and Howard, and others, were giving instructions for putting out the fire in one place, while a hundred fires were lighting all around. How much better would it have been had they brought in a division of sober troops and cleared out the town with steel and bullet. Gen. Wood's first division, 15th corps, occupied Columbia; Col Stone's brigade was the first to enter the city and hoist the flag over the Capitol—enviable notoriety had not the drunken, riotous scenes of the night sullied its honor." Is it not somewhat strange that Sherman should have been solicitous about the fire? He had told Gen. Wheeler that he would burn all the cotton, and that as to the empty houses, he paid little attention to whether they were burnt or not. We now come to the question, "Who is to blame for the burning of Columbia is a subject that will be long disputed. I know the negroes and escaped prisoners were infuriated and easily incited the inebriated soldiers to join them in their work of vandalism. Governor Magrath and Gen. Wade Hampton, are partly accountable for the destruction of their city. General Beauregard, Mayor Goodwyn and others, wanted to send a deputation as far as Orangeburgh to surrender the city, and when evacuating, to destroy all the liquors. In both of these wise views they were over-ruled by the Governor, and Wade Hampton, the latter stating that he would defend the town from house to house."

There are two points in these remarks that require to be considered. It is very evident that Conyngham believed that the returned prisoners and inebriated soldiers, were the acting agents; and that Governor Magrath, and General Hampton, were only blameable; inasmuch, as they did not surrender the city when the enemy were forty miles distant. To the grievous fault committed by the latter in not doing, we have only to say, that General Hampton had no command at the time; could have no voice in the affair; and certainly, could not have overruled the wishes of Beauregard, who was his superior, and alone in office. Moreover, the proposition never was made. I have now a letter from Mayor Goodwyn, in which he states, that no such proposition ever came before him. This is the only ground on which Conyngham attaches blame to Hampton, and I think I have shown that he had nothing to do with it, for the subject never was discussed; and so falls the allegation made by Conyngham. Had the charge against Hampton then existed, which has been subsequently made, he must have known of it. He was one of Sherman's aids—was at Headquarters—a writer for the *Herald*, and would not have omitted such news as that. His object was to gather up whatever would create a sensation.

I will add one or two more extracts from the same author, relative to Columbia, and then take the reader back to some of the scenes on the route of the army to that place, to show the *animus* with which it entered Carolina, and the determination of both officers and men, as to the course they intended to pursue; which determination was signally assisted, and strengthened by Sherman's own conduct at McBride's plantation. That whole march was characterized by such acts as we would have supposed a body of fiends let loose from Hell might have taken some pleasure in enacting; and as Nichols says in his work on the march, "you will in vain search history for a parallel."

"There can be no denial of the assertion, that the feeling of among the troops was one of extreme bitterness towards the people of the State of South Carolina. It was freely expressed as the column hurried over the bridge at Sister's ferry, eager to commence the punishment of original secessionists. Threatening words were heard from soldiers who prided themselves on conservatism in house-burning while in Georgia, and officers openly confessed their fears that the coming campaign would be a wicked one. Just or unjust as this feeling was towards the country people in South Carolina, it was universal. I first saw its fruits at Rarysburg (Purisburg is meant), where two or three piles of blackened bricks and an acre or so of dying embers marked the site of an old revolutionary town; and this before the column had fairly got its band in."[14]

"At McBride's plantation, where Gen. Sherman had his headquarters, the out-houses, offices, shanties and surroundings were all set on fire before he left. I think the fire approaching the dwelling hastened his departure. If a house was empty, this was *prima facie* evidence that the owners were rebels, and all was sure to be consigned to the flames. If they remained at home it was taken for granted that every one in South Carolina was a rebel, and the chances were the place was consumed. In Georgia few houses were burned; here few escaped, and the country was converted into one vast bonfire. The pine forests were fired; the resin factories were fired; the public buildings and dwellings were fired. The middle of the finest day looked black and gloomy, for a dense smoke arose on all sides clouding the very heavens—at night the tall pine trees seemed so many huge pillars of fire. The flames hissed and screeched, as they fed upon the fat resin and dry branches, imparting to the forest a most fearful appearance."

"Vandalism of this kind, though not encouraged, was seldom punished. True, where every one is guilty alike, there will be no informers."

"The ruined homesteads of the Palmetto State will long be remembered. The army might safely march the darkest night, the crackling pine woods shooting up their columns of flame, and the burning houses along the way would light it on, while the dark clouds and pillars of smoke would safely cover it rears. I hazard nothing in saying that three-fifths in value of the personal property of the counties we have passed through, were taken by Sherman's army. The graves were ransacked, etc. The scenes I witnessed in Columbia, were scenes that would have driven Allaric the Goth into frenzied ecstasies had he witnessed them."

---

14 This South Carolina township, better known as Purrysburg, was located on the Savannah River.

"As for the wholesale burnings, pillage, devastation, committed in South Carolina, magnify all I have said of Georgia some fifty fold, and then throw in an occasional murder, 'just to bring an old hardfisted cuss to his senses,' and you have a pretty good idea of the whole thing. Besides compelling the enemy to evacuate Charleston, we *destroyed Columbia, Orangeburg,* and *several other places,* also over fifty miles of railroad, and thousands of bales of cotton." This is a fair admission, and we might rest here and go no farther. After what he has admitted to have been done on the route, to conclude the acts of the army by saying they had destroyed Columbia was giving up the question. On his mind there could have been no doubt as to who burnt the city, and as little as to who was the cause of its being burned.

The enviable notoriety is certainly due to Sherman, and to him alone. Those who did the deed were mere agents, and acted to please a cherished commander; they all stated that they knew what Old Bill (their pet name for him) wanted, and they were determined he should be gratified.

Capt. Cornyn[15] has also hazarded an opinion as to the burning, and with but little hesitation fixes that act upon Gen. W. Hampton. He is, however, but the copyist and mere echo of Gen. Sherman, and gives no single reason why he should have placed the odium of such an act upon Gen. Hampton. He has, however, made use of some other charges tending to implicate Gen. Hampton, which alone induces me to take any notice of him here. His description is that of Sherman's *verbatim,* with a few additions and rhetorical flourishes to render it more plausible. Capt Cornyn in his letter to Archbishop Hughes thus writes: "Shortly after our columns were put in motion, the enemy beat a hasty retreat for the city, burning the bridges as they crossed the river. Here permit me to say that Gen. Hampton, on the 15th and 16th February, had it in his power to save Columbia, and to save his people from the terrible desolation that swept over their city on the night of the 17th and 18th." Again he says "had Gen. Hampton acted the part of a great captain, etc., etc., he would have proposed on the 15th and 16th to have surrendered his army, and country, to Sherman. For the promise

---

15 This was Captain John W. Cornyn (1828-1876) of the 78th Regiment, Ohio Infantry.

of protection. I am satisfied in my own mind, that Gen. Sherman would have accepted it, but Gen. Hampton pursued a different and most fratricidal course. On Thursday the 16th February, General Hampton ordered all cotton to be rolled in the streets, preparatory to burning the same." No such words are to be found in the order, but as I shall examine and reply to that part of the accusation against Hampton when I take up Sherman's charge, of which this is but the echo, I will only now say that the order alluded to by Cornyn was given on the 14th, not on the 16th, two days before Hampton was in command. For the same reason, had he been willing, he could not have proposed a surrender, and I am satisfied in my own mind, that Sherman for that reason would have taken no notice of it.

Captain Cornyn states that when he came into the town: "We found several buildings burning when we entered. The cotton in the streets was burning in many places, &c;" and again: "There were hundreds of bales of cotton in the streets from which the devouring element was hissing forth. So high was the wind that it frequently carried immense sheets of burning cotton ten and even fifteen squares through the air like a burning comet, leaving in its wake fiery devastation." I have only to say to this grandiloquent description, that it is not true. There was no house on fire when the army came in. There was but one pile of cotton burning at 12 o'clock; it was put out by one, and completely. It never blazed again, nor did a single house catch fire from it. Capt. Cornyn was entirely mistaken. There are some other errors in that letter, but they are not worth the trouble of refuting.

Major Nichols next presents himself, and as a staff officer of Gen. Sherman, we may suppose that *ego et rex meus* to be one.[16] His account is very much the counterpart of Sherman's, but he has many remarks and admissions that are peculiarly apropos to the subject, and calculated to lead one definitely to the object sought after, viz : "who is to blame for the burning of Columbia." Major Nichols remarks under the date of 30th January: "The actual invasion of South Carolina has begun. The well known sight of columns of black smoke meets our gaze again; this time *houses* are *burning,* and South Carolina

---

16   The Latin means "I and my king."

has commenced to pay an installment, long overdue, on her debt to justice and humanity. With the help of God, we will have principal and interest before we leave her borders. There is a terrible gladness in the realization of so many hopes and wishes." Again, Nichols exclaims: "But here we are; and wherever our footsteps pass, fire, ashes and desolation follow in the path." In speaking of the occupation of the city, "On every side were evidences of disorder; bales of cotton scattered here and there, articles of merchandise and furniture cast pell mell in every direction by the frightened inhabitants, &c." But no mention of anything on fire. Nichols writes: "I began to-day's record early in the evening, and while writing, I noticed an unusual glare in the sky and heard a sound of running to and fro in the streets. Running out, I found to my surprise and real sorrow," (why so after the expressions used above?) "that the central part of the city, including the main business street, was in flames, while the wind, which had been blowing a hurricane all day, was driving the sparks and cinders in heavy masses over the eastern portion of the city where the finest residences were situated. Those buildings, all wooden, were instantly ignited by the flying sparks. In half an hour the conflagration was raging in every direction, &c." It will be perceived that both Conyngham and Nichols state that the fire commenced in the evening, after dark, at the very time that Sherman states it to have been so great that he had to call in Wood's division. It will be observed also, that Conyngham, in his remarks, states "that Sherman and Howard, instead of looking after a single fire, when hundreds were burning all around, had better have called in fresh troops and driven the drunkards out with steel and lead." And again, he says, "*about day Wood's division was called on,* when nothing was left to pillage or burn." It is important to bear these facts in memory, as it will be seen that when Sherman gives an account of the catastrophe to free himself from blame, he changes the whole order of the affair and makes the fires to have been burning all day, but leaping into life and activity when the night came on, and requiring him to call for additional assistance. Nichols says "Gen. Howard and his officers worked with their own hands until long after midnight, trying to save life and property;" we presume, for the purpose of having it presented to them, as he, Nichols has so naively detailed on page 204—the manner in which silver goblets, &c., had found their way into camp.

Nichols proceeds and states: "Various causes are assigned to explain the origin of the fire. I am quite sure that it originated in sparks flying from the hundreds of bales of cotton which the rebels had placed along the middle of the main street, and fired as they left the city." This is mere assertion; no proof of the fact has been offered; the number is exaggerated, there being not more than fifty bales, and from their own statements, there is reason to believe it was not so. It is positively certain that up to half-past eleven o'clock, there had been no fire in the city; and then it had been under the command of Col. Stone for fully one hour. Again, he says: "There were fires, however, which must have been started independent of the above named cause. The source of these is ascribed to the desire for revenge from some 200 of our prisoners who h ad escaped from the cars as they were being conveyed from this city to Charlotte, &c." Again, it is said that: "the soldiers who first entered the town, intoxicated with success and a liberal supply of bad liquor, &c., set fire to unoccupied houses." There has never been any proof offered as to the cotton having been fired by Hampton's orders, or by his men. It stands alone upon the authority of Gen. Sherman's *ipse dixit*. Col. Stone, who had the best opportunity of judging of the fact, has not been appealed to and has made no such report. His evidence would have ten times the weight of Sherman's assertion, as he was the first to enter, passed through the Main street, went by the cotton and saw it, and left his men at that very spot. From thence he went to the Capitol with Alderman Stork. The men left, occupied themselves as men will do, by lounging about the cotton, laying on it and smoking, and whilst doing so, the cotton was discovered to be on fire about one hour after they had been there.

Nichols proceeds with his narrative and writes: "Houses have unquestionably been burned during our march, but they were the property of notorious rebels who were fortunate in escaping so easily; while I have yet to hear of a single instance of outrage offered to a woman or a child by any soldier of our army." We do not know what Major Nichols may consider an outrage, but for a man to catch a lady by the throat, and thrust his hand into her bosom to feel for her watch, or purse, would in former days have been regarded as such. So would the lifting up of a lady's dress, because she was not quick enough in freeing her purse from her girdle, the threats of death and a pistol at her head having alarmed her and caused her to give. I should hardly suppose that even in such an army as was led by Sherman, it would have been considered very chivalric to place a pistol at a lady's breast, and demand her watch and jewels, whilst a companion put another to the head of her daughter and demanded the same. Nor would I deem that a man entitled to admission in civilized society, who would insult the feelings of a lady by taking to a room, which he had forced from her, and opposite to her own sleeping apartment and that of her daughter, a negro woman and remain there with her all night and go off with her in the morning; yet this was done by one Capt. W. T. Duglass, a commissary, whose name was mentioned to the lady by his clerk, Mr. Sutherland, with a request that it should be published for that act, and for the theft he had been guilty of in her house as every man ought to be, who took up his quarters in a house and suffered it to be pillaged as hers had been. But what shall I say of the villain who fired the house of a lone woman, and then in the presence of her maid compelled her to be subservient to his brutal wishes?[17] Words are wanting properly to designate such an act, and we can only say it would disgraced even Butler the beast. Yet those acts were committed in many of the houses; in some instances done by officers as well as men; hence the "screams and shrieks and groans and pistol shots" that were heard by Conyngham and related by him on page 331. Still further and more wanton atrocities were committed, such as no one would repeat, and none but the lowest grade of blackguardism could have perpetrated.

So far as the Carolinian lady was concerned, much respect was shown to her person and her character. She was robbed and abused, to obtain her jewels and her money; but the instances of other injuries, though many, were not proportionate to the opportunities. The Yankee's gallantry, debauchery and brutality, were confined to

---

17 The "lone woman" likely refers to Mrs. T. B. Clarkson, whose maid was raped in her presence.

the negro; he affiliated with them; they were congenial spirits; their habits, their thoughts and their natures assimilated; they were their associates in the camp, in the streets and in the ball-room; and it was among that class, that their brutal indelicacy occurred. Neither party felt shame for what passed between them; but like the beasts of the forest, indulged in their caprices wherever they met. It was not unusual to see a Yankee soldier with his arm around the neck of a negro wench, even in the common thoroughfares, or hugging and kissing a mulatto girl, when he could find one so degraded , that she would not spurn him for his impudence and want of common decency.

I will give one extract more from Nichols and then turn to his commander who was the source from which the foul slander emanated, and see on what authority he makes his charge. "In the record of great wars we read of vast armies marching through an enemy's country, carrying death and destruction in their path; of villages burned, cities pillaged, a tribe or a nation swept out of existence. History, however, will be searched in vain for a parallel to the scathing and destructive effect of the invasion of the Carolinas." "Putting aside the mere military question for the moment, there are considerations which, overleaping the present generation, affect the future existence of the section of the country through which our army has marched!" "Over a region of forty miles in width stretching from Savannah to Port Royal through South Carolina to Goldsboro in North Carolina, agriculture and commerce, even if peace come speedily, cannot be fully revived in our day." "Day by day our legions of armed men surged over the land, destroying its substance. Cattle were gathered into increasing droves; fresh horses and mules were taken to replace the lame and feeble animals; rich granaries and store houses were stripped of corn, fodder meal and flour; cotton gins, presses, factories and mills were burned to the ground, on every side; the head, centre and rear of our column might be traced by columns of smoke by day and the glare of fires by night." "In all the length and breadth of that broad pathway the burning hand of war pressed heavily, blasting and withering where it fell." And such was the act of a band of brothers, anxious for the return of the South to the Union, to restore the friendly relations between the two sections of the country. Such were the means used to bring about fraternal concord, to reunite a mistaken people, to restore them to their pristine condition, and insure a lasting peace. It was a most extraordinary device—one worthy of Sherman from whom it emanated, but it really seems more in unison with the views of the officer who while wishing them all in hell, yet was determined to "smelt them back into the Union." Where was the Constitution they were fighting for; where the individualities of the States that had so long been cherished? Where those rights so sacred that the general government could not even purchase a piece of land without asking for and obtaining the sanction of the State? All ignore, all gone, all sunk and smelted into the one grand consolidated national government of Sherman, with more absolute power over the lives and liberty of the people than the autocrat of Russia.

From the subordinates, let me now turn to the great leader, whose word was law, and whose nod was destiny. Let us see what Sherman says as to "who is to blame for the burning of Columbia." In the frequent conversation which Sherman had with the inhabitants of the town, he uniformly attributed its destruction to the whiskey which his men obtained, and their subsequent intoxication. In no instance that I have ever heard, did he attribute it to General Hampton, nor in his letters, did he deny his complicity in the affair, until his report to the General Government; then, for the first time, we learned that General Sherman disclaimed having had anything to do with its destruction; that on the contrary, he ordered it not to be burnt. Such having been the fact, it certainly was very fortunate for the citizens of Columbia, that the General's views should have been so much misunderstood, and that all the soldiers and officers who came into the city, were under the impression it was a doomed city, and was to be given up to pillage until night; and then at a signal given, it was to be burnt. Such undoubtedly was the prevailing opinion, and a nervous restlessness was to be observed about them, an anxious looking out for an expected event, which they instantly recognized and hailed when the rockets were thrown up, and immediately proceeded to their task. That General Sherman had given, his orders to General Howard, to burn all the public buildings, by which he meant all that had been used in Confederate service, he himself, acknowledges. That he did so before he entered the town, or became acquainted with their position, is also certain; that they were so situated, their cremation would end in one general conflagration, was patent to every one, and the order given for their destruction was, as a matter of course, an order for the destruction of the city; that General Sherman gave that order he has himself recorded; but in no place has he shown where the order ever was countermanded, or where regarding the safety of the city he had guaranteed, with such a wind as was blowing, that he sought the means to prevent the catastrophe. From the statement of his officers, it was certain that he could have prevented it. It was certain that he made no effort to do so—and absolutely certain that he allowed the very corps who had exhibited the greatest animosity, and uttered the most violent threats to enter the city, remain in it when drunk, and continue there until its destruction was completed, or as Conyngham writes "until there was nothing more to pilfer or burn." The same men who were detailed to destroy it, entered with the belief that it would be peculiarly agreeable to him, as General Howard says. They stated such to be their intention. Stated that their orders were on the appearance of a certain signal, the rockets, that they were to fire and pillage, and continue until the bugle's sound countermanded the orders, and called in the incendiaries. Such were the facts stated by hundreds of the soldiers, and officers as early as 12 o'clock in the day, and such were the facts that developed themselves on the approach of the evening. General Sherman in his remarks to the Secretary of War, endeavours to exculpate himself, and to fix the terrible accident on another. It is my object, now, to state the charge of the General, and to show to the world that it was not true; and that from all the incidents previous, and subsequent to his entrance into Columbia, he himself and no other was the cause of the destruction of the city of Columbia.

He writes: "In anticipation of the occupation of the city, I had made written orders to General Howard touching the conduct of the troops. These were to destroy absolutely all arsenals and public property not needed for our own use, as well as railroads, depots and machinery, useful in war to an enemy; but to spare all dwellings, colleges, schools, asylum and harmless property. I was the first to cross the pontoon-bridge, and in company with General Howard rode into the city. The day was clear, but a perfect tempest of wind was raging. The brigade of Colonel Stone was already in the city and was properly posted. Citizens and soldiers were on the streets, and general good order prevailed. General Wade Hampton, who commanded the Confederate rear guard of cavalry, had in anticipation of the capture of Columbia, ordered that all cotton, public and private, should be moved into the streets and fired, to prevent our making use of it. Bales were piled everywhere, the rope and bagging cut, and tufts of cotton were blown about in the wind, lodged in the trees and against houses, so as to resemble a snow storm. Some of these piles of cotton were burning especially, one in the very heart of the city, near the Court House, but the fire was partially subdued by the labors of our soldiers. Before one single public building had been fired by order, the smouldering fires set by Hampton's orders were rekindled by the wind and communicated to the buildings around. About dark, they began to spread and got beyond the control of the brigade on duty within the city. The whole of Woods' division was brought in, but it was found impossible to check the flames, which, by midnight became unmanageable, and raged until about 4 a.m., when the wind subsiding, they were got under control." "I was up nearly all night, and saw Generals Howard, Logan, Wood and others, laboring to save houses, etc., etc." "I disclaim on the part of my army any agency in this fire, but on the contrary, claim that we saved what of Columbia remains unconsumed. And without hesitation, I charge General Wade Hampton with having burned his own city of Columbia, not with a malicious intent, or as the manifestation of a silly "Roman stoicism," but from folly and want of sense, in filling it with lint, cotton and tinder. Our officers and men on duty worked well to extinguish the flames; but others not on duty, including the officers who had long been imprisoned there, rescued by us, may have assisted in spreading the fire, and may have indulged in unconcealed joy to see the ruins of the capital of South Carolina."

I have already alluded to the orders given to General Howard in anticipation of the taking of the city, and of the reckless and wanton destruction of property that must arise therefrom, and not being acquainted with the position of the houses which were thus doomed to destruction—one of which, the Central Bureau, the third house fired, was ignited by Yankee soldiers, and put out and was again fired, and was the cause of the destruction of the whole block. It was near a large dry goods store and drug establishment, which were also fired at the same time, by a Yankee soldier furnished with combustibles. This Bureau was one of the buildings ordered by Sherman to be fired, and for this purpose several men were detailed. They waited for the signal, and in ten minutes after it was given, the place was in flames. It was impossible that this building could have been fired by the cotton; it was to the northward and westward of the cotton, with a hurricane blowing from t he northwest. About the same time, the house of Mr. Jacob Bell was set fire to and burned. This house was at least five squares to the northward and eastward, and it also was safe from the cotton, but not from the turpentine carried about by the incendiaries. There is no evidence that the order for burning was recalled, and Gen. Howard acknowledged that the troops were under the impression that Sherman wished the city destroyed. I will refer to this hereafter. Sherman says "the brigade of Col. Stone was already in the city and properly posted—citizens and soldiers were in the street together, and general good order prevailed." Except in their stealing, such was the fact and continued so until after dark when rockets were discharged, and then the whole scene changed. (See Conyngham's and Nichols' account of the conduct of the troops &c., at that time.) What was it that changed the orderly soldier obedient to his commander, to the midnight assassin, robber and house-burner? Three rockets discharged—the signal agreed on when as the soldiers said "Hell was to be let loose and the city wrapped in flames." But let me take Sherman up in the order of his report. "Gen. Hampton who commanded etc., ordered that all cotton should be moved in the streets and fired to prevent our making use of it."

In his letter to Rawls, Sherman says that in the printed order which he saw, Hampton ordered "that on the approach of the Yankee army all the cotton should be burned." This order which he says he saw, and worded as above is the proof he offers of Gen. Hampton having burned the town. He has no other. It is the ground of the whole charge, and the one on which all his allegations are founded. Were I to grant that an order had been given by Hampton, it would become necessary for Gen. Sherman to prove that the one he had named was the identical one; and that it gave the direction, and authority to act, which Sherman states; but I am not disposed to cede so much, and I think it can be made apparent, though in his name, that the order did not emanate from him—that he sought to have it countermanded, succeeded in doing so, and had it stopped. That order is dated.

HEADQUARTERS, Feb. 14, 1865

[Special Order No. -----]

All persons having cotton stored in the city of Columbia, are directed to have it placed where it can be burned in case of necessity, without danger of destroying buildings. All cotton stored here will be burned at any cost rather than allow it to fall in the hands of the enemy.

By order of

Major Gen. HAMPTON

R. Lowndes, Capt. and A. A. G.

Feb. 15th

I think it will be difficult to show in that order, any directions to roll the cotton into the streets, or to fire it upon the approach of the Yankee army. It contains nothing of the kind; it is a precautionary order to be acted on if a necessity should occur. General Sherman was too well acquainted with what was transpiring in the army of opponent, not to know that Gen. Hampton at the time that order was given was not in command—that order is dated on the 14th. Gen. Hampton was put in command on the night of the 16th; he therefore could have had no authority to issue such a one; he was only assisting Beauregard. How that order was printed in his name I know not, and cannot therefore speak. I presume it could be explained, but for my purposes it is not necessary. It unquestionably is not such an order as Sherman stated that he saw—no rolling into the streets—and by it no one was authorized to fire the cotton. It was one of precaution, to be acted on under a contingency, and of that contingency Gen. Hampton was to be the judge. No authority was given to any one to burn it, nor could it have been burnt but by the order of Hampton, who was to judge of the necessity. That he did not issue that order is to my mind very plain, for if he had done so, he would have had the same power that gave the order, to authorize him to withdraw it; but it seems he felt that he had not, for immediately upon taking his command as Lieut. General, he applied to Beauregard to get the order countermanded, as will be seen by the following correspondence. Gen. Hampton writes to Gen. Beauregard as follows:

April 22, 1866

Gen. Sherman having charged me in his official report with the destruction of Columbia, and have reiterated the same falsehood in a recent letter to Benj. Rawls of that city, may I beg you to state such facts in reference to this matter as are in your possession. If you recollect, I advised you on the morning the Yankees came in, not to burn the cotton as this would endanger the town. I stated that as they had destroyed the railroad they could not remove the cotton. Upon this representation you directed me to issue an order that the cotton should not be burned. This I did at once, and there was not a bale on fire when the Yankees came into the town. You saw the cotton as you left the city, and you can state that none was on fire. Very respectfully yours. W. H.

To Gen. Beauregard

To which Gen. Beauregard returned the following answer endorsed on the letter:

N. O., May 2, 1866

The above statement of Gen. Hampton relative to the order issued by me at Columbia, S.C., not to burn the cotton in that city is perfectly true and correct. The only thing on fire at the time of the evacuation was the depot building of the S.C.R.R., which caught fire accidentally from the explosion of some ammunition ordered to be sent towards Charlotte, N.C.

G. T. Beauregard

Evidence such as this ought to be sufficient to exonerate Hampton from all agency in the burning of the cotton. The fact that he asked Beauregard to countermand the order, evidences that he himself had not authority to do so; and if he had no authority to countermand, certainly he could have had none to order. His asking for that power destroys the validity of the whole charge. But is the order such as Sherman states it? I think not. It gave authority to no one to burn the cotton. That the cotton was not on fire when Generals Beauregard and Hampton left Columbia is now stated; and the Mayor testifies that when he left the city to go and meet Sherman there was no fire of any kind in the city; and he testifies to the fact that when he came back with Colonel Stone the cotton was not then on fire. Aldermen McKenzie and Stork both testify to the same, and Stork says that he saw the Yankee soldiers light their segars and throw the matches in among the cotton. Upon McKenzie's pointing out cotton to Captain Pratt, and that very pile, Captain Pratt remarked, "I wish you would had burnt the whole; it would have saved us trouble, as our orders are to burn all the cotton in the town." Had the cotton been on fire Pratt would have noticed and spoken of it. Alderman McKenzie, who was the Captain of one of the Fire Companies, states that it was some time after his return with Stone and Pratt before the cotton was on fire, and when the alarm was given was given he proceeded to the place, and never left it until the fire was perfectly extinguished, and the cotton so soaked that it could not again blaze out. Alderman Stork says the same, and adds, moreover, that even the conflagration of the night had not been able to burn it, for it was laying there for some days after. Some was then removed and the rest trodden down and incorporated into the ground. There are hundreds of witnesses to the same fact.

The Rev. Mr. Shand[18] was present when the cotton took fire and I will quote what he says in a letter to me on the subject, and then leave that part of it as settled: "There was a row of cotton bales which *had been loosely packed*, and from almost all of which portions of the fabric were protruding. Along this line of bales there were numbers of Yankee soldiers, *and none but they*—the citizens who were present

---

18   Reverend Peter J. Shand was minister of Trinity Episcopal Church in Columbia.

being confined to the pavements on each side of the street, and at a distance of from thirty to forty feet or more from the cotton. The soldiers were passing to and fro, alongside of the bales, apparently in a state of high excitement, and almost frantic with joy; all, or most of them, with lighted segars in their mouths. I was standing nearly midway between the two corners, watching their movements, when on a sudden the bale at the market end took fire, and the wind being quite fresh, the flames increased and spread with fearful rapidity, and in a short time the whole, or at least the greater part, was in a blaze. The fire engines of the city were brought to the spot as expeditiously as possible and the fire was extinguished in the course of an hour. It was evident that it originated from the fire of the cigars, falling upon the loose cotton. Indeed there was no other way of accounting for it; and another thing is to be noted, that neither sparks nor flames were extended to the neighboring buildings and no damage was done except to the cotton."

I will continue the narrative of this gentleman as it runs on to the events of the night; since he details clearly the circumstances which occurred and to which he was an eye witness. I have thus fairly shown that General Hampton gave no such order to fire the cotton as Sherman states, nor was its burning attributable to any of his men, or the citizens; but, that it originated from the acts of Sherman's own men, and probably from the very ones who had been detailed for the purpose, and felt that they were performing an acceptable service to their General. I will also state here a part of the conversation which took place between General Howard and Mr. Shand on the burning of Columbia, to which I have elsewhere allude, and will use the very words spoken. General Howard expressed his regret at the occurrence and added the following words: "Though General did not order the burning of the town, yet somehow or other the men had taken up the idea that if they destroyed the capital of South Carolina, it would be peculiarly gratifying to General Sherman." Mr. Shand continues: "The fire was wholly put out by one o'clock P.M., and from that hour until 7 and 8 o'clock P.M., there was no other fire in the city, and the burning of said cotton, therefore, had nothing to do with the subsequent conflagration and destruction of the town. At the hour last mentioned rockets were seen to ascend and immediately thereafter a fire broke out in a central portion of the city near the market, and the wind being exceedingly high, it soon assumed alarming proportions. I stood in my front piazza watching it with much anxiety and though inclined at first to regard its origin as accidental, I was soon undeceived. The fire occurred, as I said, in the central part of the city and to the north of my residence, but I had been looking upon it for but a short time when I noticed fresh flames bursting out in the east, west and south, at points *very distant* from each other and not possibly caused by the communication of flames from one to the other. The revelry of soldiers in the streets and their shouts and exultation, as fresh rockets went up, and fresh buildings took fire, scenes which t some extent came under my own observation, added to the awful character of the occasion and gave rise to the painful impression that the city was doomed to desolation and ruin; a fact which was admitted and boasted of by some of the soldiers themselves. By midnight the whole city presented one vast sheet of flames, and in the midst, and during the progress of the appalling calamity, might be heard above all other noises, the demoniac and gladsome shouts of the soldiery." He further speaks of efforts made to burn his house, their success and their brutal treatment of himself and robbery of the church plate, &c.

Let us follow out Sherman's report. "Bales were piled everywhere, the rope and bagging cut," (no proof of any such being the case) "and tufts of cotton were blown about in the wind, lodged in the trees, and against houses, so as to resemble a snow storm." This is very poetical, and might give him credit for descriptive powers, but it is too fanciful, and moreover, was not true; after all, it is but a sketch of the imagination. That cotton, which in his eye was flying about in flakes, and adorning the houses with their tufts, was so soaked and sodden, that it did not even burn from the heat of the conflagration of the night, and remained for days on the ground, until it was incorporated with it "by being constantly trodden underfoot." He says "the fire was partially put out by our soldiers;" so far as their labor was concerned, that might be. General Sherman entirely ignores the action of our own firemen with their engines, who did the work, and did it thoroughly. It never blazed forth again, though he writes that "Before one single public building had been fired by order, the smouldering fires set by Hampton's orders, were rekindled by the wind, and communicated to the buildings around."

I have already shown that Hampton gave no orders, and McKenzie and Stork certify that the fires did not again kindle, nor was a house ignited by the cotton—but that the houses contiguous to it, were fired in the rear by Yankee soldiers, who were seen to do so by most credible witnesses. No building was fired from the cotton, nor was it possible for it to have communicated with the first house in flames that night, or to dozens of others which shared the same fate. The pile of cotton which Sherman saw, and to which he alludes, was in Richardson street, near the market, was extinguished by 1 o'clock, and never again ignited. The first fire took place on Gervais or Bridge street, near Gates street, and occurred immediately after the firing of the rockets. Those rockets were considered to be the signal for destruction; which was anxiously waited for, and promptly attended to. The houses in Gervais street were the first fired in the city. No fire had occurred after 1 o'clock P.M.

Hampton's, Wallace's, Mrs. Stark's, etc., burnt early in the afternoon; they were in the country, and two miles from the cotton—a fact which beg the reader to bear in mind. The house on Gervais street was about 500 yards to the southwest of the cotton, and a hurricane as Cornyn says, was blowing. The wind was from the northwest. Under such circumstances it was a physical impossibility for fire to have been communicated. On the contrary, a Yankee was seen to fire it, as well as others adjoining. The next house burnt was that of Bates' and Oliver's, which was near the cotton. No cotton was on fire then. The house was fired in the rear, in Oliver's shoe shop, and put out by a negro who was in charge of the building. The Yankee soldier ordered him to desist or he would beat him. He then fired the house completely, and was seen to do it by several citizens who testified to the fact. The next building was the so-called public property—the Central Bureau for distributing clothing to the soldiers who were in want. Phillips' ware-house was fired about the same time. This was a block to the north, and the flames could not have ignited, as they would have had to travel against the wind. Then followed Bell's house, five squares off to the north, and east of the others. These premises were all seen to be fired by the Yankee soldiers carrying combustibles; and not one was so observed until after the signal had been given; not a fire occurred from the cotton, Sherman's assertion to the contrary notwithstanding. After these, fires were to be seen blazing in every direction in the town, and occurring so rapidly one after the other, as to leave no doubt that it was a simultaneous movement, and done by men regularly instructed as to their duty. I could multiply any number of special incidents to prove that the firing was systematic, and consequently ordered. A building, fire-proof on the outside, was being fired within and put out, when the guard told the owner it was no use to struggle against it, as "his house was doomed and had to go." Another, upon removing the fire brand which was put between his floors, was told "to let it alone;" that "the damned house was to burn—it was on the black list."

"About dusk the fires began to spread and got beyond the control of the brigade on duty within the city." That is true after the rockets were thrown up—somewhere about eight o'clock at night when the fires spread with great rapidity, but no effort was made by the Yankees to arrest the conflagration. The engines were taken from their captains, and so injured as to be useless. The hose was cut, as testified to by Captains Stanley and McKenzie of the fire companies of the city, and the town lay helpless before them; but not a move was made by the Yankees to check the progress of the flames except where a house was burning contiguous to where their officers were staying. Then it would be arrested. Such was the case with Dr. Leland's residence. It was contiguous to Gen. Sherman's headquarters and I think where Col. Stone was stationed. They saved that house, while that of a widowed lady, Mrs. Levy, was permitted to burn by its side—probably because the destruction of Dr. Leland's house would throw the officers out of comfortable quarters. Sherman says "the whole of Wood's Division was brought in, but it was found impossible to check the flames which by midnight h ad become unmanageable and raged until about 4 A.M., when the wind subsiding, they were got under control." All correct, except one little item, viz: that Wood's division was not called in until about three and four, and they did not fail, but arrested it immediately. Gen. Sherman as been very forgetful of hours in this statement; Wood's division was not called in until morning, and their being called in arose from a little incident which I will presently mention. Conyngham bears me out in the assertion. He says "this scene continued until near morning, and then the town was cleared out, when there was nothing more to pillage or burn." Sherman says, "I was up nearly all night, and saw Gens. Howard, Logan, Wood and others, laboring to save houses etc." I do not question that there were many circumstances calculated to render Sherman's rest disturbed, but why he and Howard and Logan and Wood should have tried to save houses rather mystifies me. Sherman had ordered the place to be burnt—Howard was carrying it out—Logan was in favor of the measure, and after he had left Columbia, declared if it was to be done again, that he would do it more effectually. He also ordered Preston's house to be destroyed. Wood, it would seem, had the command of the forces about the town; and the Yankee writers state, could have prevented, or have arrested it at any time had he thought proper. That Sherman should be disturbed was perhaps natural; he was not quite demon, and the act he had just authorized was fiendish, though it seem to give him gratification. His officers spoke freely of his disregard for the condition of the city, and declared without hesitation that he could have prevented it, and could then (two o'clock) stop it by calling in fresh troops, and driving out the drunken soldiers who were disgracing the army.

Between three and four, an incident occurred which led to his ordering in fresh troops, and arresting the conflagration. Then, and not till then, was Wood's division ordered in. Eight hours after the time he stated to the Secretary of War that he had called them in, they came in, turned out the rioters, and removed the incendiaries. The incident tended much to show the feelings of Sherman, and the course that he had been pursuing. Whilst wandering about the city and admiring the sublimity of the terrible scene, he was recognized by a lady and accosted. She pointed out to him the devastation going on and endeavored to enlist his feelings by showing the desolation that must follow, and the misery that must overtake s many homeless, destitute families. He told her he had nothing to do with it; that he had not ordered it; that it was her own people who had left whiskey in their way, and given it to the soldiers. She replied, if you have not ordered it, common humanity should impel you to arrest it. He replied, he could not, the wind was so high. She then said, you can stop your men from continuing to fire it; he denied that his men had anything to do with it;

that it was our own fault. Whilst making this denial, a servant came up and informed her mistress that a man was setting fire to the kitchen. Sherman asked where, she pointed to him, and he ordered him shot. The guard fired, but the incendiary did not fall, and he caught him and brought him to Sherman who asked if he had not ordered him to shoot him. The man replied, you did, but I did not think you meant me to kill him. There it stopped. The man was ordered to the guard house. He was only performing the duty assigned him; but in the wrong place and time. His fellow soldier knew he was authorized to do what he was then doing, and so told his commander that he did not think he wanted him killed. After this incident, Sherman gave orders to Capt. Andrews to have the fire arrested, and I beg the reader to remark the words that were used. I have heard the circumstances told by several who knew of it, and from those who were present, and all used the same terms of expression. Addressing Capt. Andrews, Sherman said: "This thing has gone far enough. See that a stop is put to it; take Wood's Division, and I hold you and them responsible, if it is not arrested." Let us analyze this order. "This thing has gone far enough." Does not that imply that he was aware of what was going on, and that it met with his sanction. "See that a stop is put to it." Doe not that he knew it could be stopped? "I hold you and them responsible if it is not arrested." Certainly this shows that he knew it was under his control, and all the statements made of his inability to stop it, and his regret, &c., proved to have been merely a deception. Sherman says that "about dark the fires began to spread, and got beyond control, &c." At that time there was not a fire in the city, nor did they begin until near eight o'clock after the signal rockets had been thrown up, and then simultaneously in every direction of the city, the houses were to be seen in a blaze. That Sherman ordered the destruction of the city, his soldiers did not hesitate to aver. As soon as they came in, they stated that the city would be burned. That it was settled on the other side of the river between the officers and themselves. That a signal would be given, and then the citizens would "see hell." General Sherman says he disclaims "on the part of my army, any agency in this fire;" but on the contrary claims, that "we saved what of Columbia remained unconsumed."

After the facts which I have just stated, I think it will be difficult for any one to give credit to the disclaimer. But as to the saving of what is left of Columbia unconsumed, there is no question that he is entitled to that credit, for after the signal rockets, and until Wood's Division was called in, between three and four in the morning, the city was burning with fearful rapidity; while after the order was given to Andrews, and the bugles sound called the incendiaries from their work of infamy, all became changed. The fire was arrested; no more houses were ignited; and the destruction of the place ceased. Sherman therefore did put an end to the fire, and certainly saved, by his order, "the remnant of the once rich and flourishing city." But subsequent events tended to show that he regretted his fit of benevolence. There can be but little doubt that there was an intention to burn the balance when they left; McGregor's house was fired at four o'clock P.M. on Saturday. Latta's and English's were destroyed on Sunday. Preston's house was ordered for the closing scene on Monday, as soon as General Logan should leave; and its destruction was only prevented by an accidental circumstance. Major Fitzgibbon, who felt interested in the condition of the nuns, called on and asked if he could assist them. They stated that they had Sherman's promise of protection. He inquired if it was in writing' they replied no, it was only a verbal promise. He urged them to have a written one offered and to carry their request if they would write a letter to Sherman. He was so urgent, and as he stated that night would be one of horrors, that they wrote to General Sherman; Fitzgibbon carried the note, and brought them back a written protection, together with guards for their property. His language indicated his belief that the destruction of the city would be effected that night. Sherman's protection, however, did not assist them. Their establishment was destroyed, and they, and their helpless charge of young girls, spend the night in the church yard. Some ladies seeing their condition, called on Sherman, represented their condition, and urged upon him to render them assistance. He called in the morning, saw the Mother Superior, expressed his deep regret at their loss, and troubled condition, stated that it arose from no act of his, that the conflagration resulted from the liquor which his soldiers had obtained; that they had become intoxicated and unmanageable; and concluded by offering to give them any house in Columbia they might choose to select for their establishment.

He desired his Adjutant Col. Charles Ewing to attend to their wants and see that they were made comfortable. That gentleman called often and tried to render their situation more pleasant, and on the eve of his departure, he introduced Captain Cornyn, the Commissary, to them, who was to arrange with them as to their rations. In the course of the conversation, Ewing reminded them of Gen. Sherman's offer to give them any house they would select and urged them to accept it; they replied they had thought of it, and would select Gen. Preston's house as being the largest in the town. Ewing replied "that is where Gen. Logan holds his Headquarters; and that house is ordered to be burned. I know that it will be burned tomorrow; but, if you will say that you will take it, I will see the General (he was Sherman's brother-in-law) and get the order countermanded." On the next morning, Captain Cornyn called and told the nuns that the army was moving in haste, and that General Sherman had left the city about four in the morning. They asked if he could tell them whether the order to burn the house had been countermanded, or one given for them to take possession. He could not. After many inquiries, they found that Gen. Perry had command of the place, and that his orders were to burn the house at a certain hour, unless they the nuns were in absolute possession; but he sent them word, if but a part of them came in, he would spare it for their sake. Two of them moved in, and found the fires all prepared, and everything in readiness to burn or blow up the building. The negroes were moving out the bedding, blankets, &c., before it should be destroyed. Here then is rather positive proof that Gen. Sherman paid no respect to his pledge concerning private property. He had pledged himself to the Mayor that person and property should be respected, but here, two days after they had held the city, without any reason that could be assigned, he orders a large and costly house to be burnt, simply because he had the power to show his authority and vent his spleen. Other houses were burnt at the time that was ordered to be destroyed, and we have reason, therefore, to suppose that the man who ordered the one, had also given directions for the other.

It will be seen above that Sherman stated to the nuns that his army was under the influence of liquor, and demoralized. Such was not the fact. The discipline was perfect, and the obedience of the army to the officers exemplary. They never were freed from his control; never interfered with each other, and when taken in hand, that discipline was exemplified in their prompt attention to the orders given to Andrews. Their discipline was never relaxed, but certain men were freed from it for special purposes, etc., and it was this freedom that enabled them to commit with impunity all the atrocities of the night; saved them from the patrol, as Conyngham states, and enabled John Hays, of Kilpatrick's cavalry, to go into the country and burn Hampton's establishment. This man stopped at a house to enquire the way, stated his reasons for wanting to know, and remarked that it was his ambition and the dearest wish of his heart to burn Hampton's home. On his return, he called and told the ladies he had effected his purpose. It was this freedom that enabled them to burn up Wallace's, Stark's and Trenholm's residences. We presume that Millwood, Woodlands, and Trenholm's Mills and quarters—places burnt two days after the general conflagration—were also destroyed by special order.

But leaving the city now to repose in its ashes, let us follow Sherman in his career through the country. From Columbia to Blackstocks, there was scarcely a dwelling left. Houses, barns, ricks, shanties, fences, ploughs, all shared the same fate, while the carcasses of horses, mules, cows, hogs, sheep, strewed the earth; killed in the most barbaric wantonness of power. Sherman's advent to Winnsboro, ended in its destruction, but in his report to the Government he does not allude to its being burnt. Thereby, perhaps, hangs a tale. The why and how might have been demanded, and perhaps he doubted whether Slocum would be civil enough to let him account for it in his own manner. It is certain that whilst Slocum held it, it suffered no detriment. He had pledged himself that it should be protected. It is equally certain that after Sherman arrived there, a considerable part of it was burnt, and not by Slocum's order.

In concluding his account of the burning of Columbia, he reiterates his assertion that it had been done by Hampton, and then goes on to laud his officers and men for their efforts to save the city. He speaks of those on duty, working "well to extinguish the flames," but whilst the army, with its left hand, are making a show of effort, with its right he acknowledges that it was scattering destruction. "Others, not on duty, including the officers who had long been imprisoned, rescued by us, may have assisted in spreading the fire after it had once begun, and may have indulged in unconcealed joy to see the ruin of the Capitol of South Carolina."

Let us now review the assertions of the men and officers to their orders and intentions when they entered Columbia. We have become acquainted with their object and views on their route to the city. We have seen the woods on fire and the houses in flames, to light them on their way, the cattle killed and the property stolen. The more dark and hidden deeds they have thrown a veil over, but let us see what was the fate destined for Columbia. The Rev. Wm. Yates states: "I was in the yard when that fatal rocket went up and one of the men exclaimed "now you will see hell." I asked him what it meant, and his reply was: *'That is the signal for a general setting of fire to the city,'* and immediately after, numbers of fires could be seen in every direction." This was at Gen. Blair's headquarters and from one of his men. Mr. Shand saw them attempt to fire one of his out houses, and saw them destroy the cotton. Mr. Oliver saw them set fire to Mrs. Law's house, turn Mr. Reckling's wife and child out of his home, and fire it, and also witnessed them firing the cotton. Alderman Stork saw them fire the cotton in the street and also witnessed the destruction of Bates' and Oliver's house. They told Captain Stanley that they would "give them Hell tonight;" that they would burn the city, and that the arrangements were all made over the river before they came in. Capt. S. was the captain of one of the fire companies, and whilst working at the fire in the rear of the Commercial Bank, fifteen or twenty armed soldiers forcibly took possession of the hoses, stuck their bayonets into them, carried off the pipes, and beat in the air vessel of the engine. He saw soldiers set fire to the Mutual supply association store. Capt. Pratt who came in with the Mayor and Col. Stone, told Alderman McKenzie, who showed him some cotton, that he wished he had burnt it and saved them the trouble as they "never left any of that." Mr. McKenzie as captain of one of the fire companies worked at the burning cotton about half past eleven, and continued to do so, until it was completely extinguished. He also assisted in arresting the fire at the jail, which he thinks was fired by one of the inmates. His firm conviction is, that the city was fired by Sherman's men and through his directions. Mr. Bedell states that the Yankees set fire to his dwelling house, and that all he could do, could not prevent them from effecting their purpose of burning it. Mrs. McDonald saw the Yankee soldiers break open Mr. Pelham's door and fire his house; Mrs. Squires saw the teamsters set fire to the cotton opposite DeSaussure's; she and he family put it out; that was about half past five in the afternoon. She saw the rockets go up, and immediately after, fires were to be seen in every direction. She confirms what others state, that Bates' and Oliver's establishments were fired in the rear, and, therefore, from those houses spread to the opposite side of the street. Her own house was fired by cotton steeped in turpentine, placed on rods and put upon the roof. Mrs. Friedeberg's house and DeSaussure's were all fired about the same time. Mr. Altee says he saw the Yankee soldiers going about and firing the houses on Bridge street and near his own—they twice fired his, but he was fortunate enough to get it extinguished. In one case, it is probable that the enemy would have added murder to their other crimes. A sergeant and three privates went to the residence of F. G. de Fontaine, Esq., the editor of the *Daily South Carolinian*, and demanded of the servants where he was to be found. The latter being unable to give the information, one of the men replied—Damn him, it is well for him that he isn't here, for we'd burn him in his den. Then, after ransacking the library, papers, etc., with a lighted candle they ignited the wood work on the place and left it to burn. Subsequently two Federal soldiers were found burned to death among the ruins of the South Carolinian office, in another part of the city. Mr. Pelham, the editor of the *Guardian,* was likewise threatened with death in case of capture. I need quote no more. I deem this sufficient to prove that the Yankee soldiers fire the cotton and the houses. Now let us see what they declared to be their intentions. Hundreds of them said to others as was said to Stanley, that they were at liberty to do as they pleased in the town, and intended to burn it to the ground. Two officers, one of the 15th, and the other of the 17th corps, stated, that "they and the soldiers were at liberty to do whatever they pleased; the only restriction was not to injure the women and children." Mrs. Thompson states that her guard told her that before morning there would be no need of a guard for her property as it would be all gone. A captain from Ohio asked her why she had stayed in Columbia; said "it was a doomed city; that Sherman had given orders to his troops upon crossing the river, that they were first to sack the city, and then burn it when the signal should be given viz: three rockets." Mr. Thompson states that he was a member of the fire company; that there was no fire in the town when Stone came in; that the fires commenced after the signals, and that the soldiers told him they "always meant to burn it." Lieut. McCroney when conversing with Mr. Harris expressed great admiration of Sherman, and remarked that "he would soon bring the war to a termination; that his policy was to destroy everything by fire and sword in his line of march, and especially Columbia, which he had determined on long before he marched here." A gentleman of Columbia called upon Sherman on the night of the fire to get a guard for the protection of his family and house which was much exposed. He could not see Sherman, but met with Capt. Merrill, who told him that Sherman had given orders to admit no one, and that his seeing him would make no difference, for "Sherman did not care a damn if the whole city was in ashes." I will now bring this article to a close, after making a few remarks on the burning of the gas works by Gen. Howard under, I must say, the express orders of Gen. Sherman, for such it had every appearance to have been. Mr. Jas. G. Gibbes heard that the gas works were to be burnt. As this was altogether private property, could have no bearing on the conduct of the war and was not a building useful in war to an enemy; as Gen. Sherman had promised protection to all private property—colleges, schools, harmless houses, etc., it was thought that such an establishment ought not to be injured, and that having deprived the citizens of their arms, wood, water, provisions and every means of procuring them by the burning of all the mills, and the stealing of all the wagons and horses, they might at least have light spared to them, to enable them to take care of their children who had been so cruelly thrown out of their homes, and deprived of every necessary. This gentleman hearing that Gen. Howard had the ordering of its destruction went to him, and remonstrated with him upon the cruelty of such a measure; depicted the distress it would occasion, and the utter wantonness of destroying such a building. Howard replied that he saw no reason why that should not be burnt as well as the other buildings. He was then requested to postpone its firing until Sherman could be appealed to; he told him he would see Sherman himself; the gentleman asked permission to go with him, as he Gen. H. being in favor of burning, he would not be likely to prove a warm advocate; he declined permission, but said he would see Sherman and try and get the order countermanded. After such a promise we presume he did call on Sherman and endeavor to change his determination. The gas works were however burnt, and we have a right to presume that Sherman gave the order for their destruction, and refused to countermand it. He therefore violated his pledge of protection to the citizen and his property, and committed an act of as wanton destruction as ever was done by man. The burning of those works, the order to burn Preston's house, the destruction of Mrs. English's, Latta's, and hosts of other houses and the utter devastation of the whole country from Columbia to North Carolina, makes him one of the most ruthless invaders that ever cursed the earth by his presence. Attila or Alaric shrink into insignificance when compared with him; and Nichols was right in saying "that will in vain search history for a parallel to the scathing and destructive effect of the invasion of the Carolinas." I have elsewhere shown that neither Sherman nor any of his officers had attributed the burning of the city to aught else than the inebriation of the soldiers; and up to the 4th of April, the date of his report to the Secretary of War, no accusation had been made against Hampton. That was the charge the charge then brought forward was an afterthought, all the antecedents tend to prove. He spoke of the burning as arising from the intoxication of his men—yet on his route through the country, *after* leaving Columbia, he carried out the system he commenced at the bridges below, and kept up during his march to the capital. In his letter to Wheeler, he avows his intention to burn all the cotton, and also his utter disregard as to what became of the dwellings of the planters. To talk of empty houses was ridiculous; from necessity, those houses could have no occupants, though the furniture and slaves evidenced their being cared for, and in fact inhabited. In his letter to Hampton of the 27th of February, relative to the prisoners being shot, &c., he makes no allusion to Columbia; and when Hampton replied, denying all knowledge of any prisoners who were shot after having been taken, he charges Sherman with having burned the city of Columbia after he had peaceable possession of it, and of other matters contrary to the usage of civilized nations. To this charge, Gen. Sherman never replied. At that time he, the great conqueror, never dreamed of being assailed; but, to his astonishment, he found the reverse. At that time he rather looked upon the burning of Columbia as the crowning act of his glory, and for the destruction of our capital he expected something like deification; nor did he awake from his delusion until the rude act of the Secretary of War aroused him from his reverie, and he began to think that he had carried his desire of vengeance too far, and that it would be advisable that some cause should be shown to Government why such an atrocity had been perpetrated. It was then he thought of the order he had seen, made his arrangements accordingly, and became satisfied that the city was fully on fire before he gave the order to burn it down through the destruction of the public buildings. Posterity will not be as blind as the present race; their passions will not be excited, and they will acknowledge that Carolina fought, and nobly fought, for a right that she and all the States were entitled to, and had ever claimed; and that, in the infamous desire to crush out her love of liberty and State sovereignty, a tiger had been unchained, who had revelled in blood and destruction, and still continued, and probably would rule until nothing was left of liberty or civil rights to the consolidated but enslaved nation.

I have now done with General Sherman. I trust that I have answered Conyhnham's question which I set out ato do; that I have removed the slander attempted to be cast on Gen. Hampton by Sherman and his satellites; proved that Tecumseh Sherman was the incendiary; and he, and he alone, is responsible for the terrible destruction that had been occasioned, and the retarding of prosperity for the next fifty years. To his God I now leave the miserable wretch, in the full belief that he will meet with such punishment as his atrocious acts have merited.

Having finished with Gen. Sherman and his *fetes* of arson, let me turn to advent few remarks of Major Nichols, in which, contrary to good taste, as well as civility and truth, he attempts to libel the character of the Carolinians. Let me review the statements and the comments he has ventured to indulge in and I think they will tend fully to portray not only a vile animus, but a miserable baseness of mind. I cannot leave the subject without exhibiting some of his wondrous qualities and gifts.

A portion of what he narrates, he has seen and heard. But when he gives such a description of Hampton, as he was done on page 311, we are compelled to say that he was not acquainted with the man. Of all persons whom I have ever known, and I have known him since infancy, he is the most uniform and imperturbable in his temper. No one ever saw him give way to passion; his face is one of remarkable quietude and repose, and he is rather reticent than otherwise. In his manner there is a calmness and severity that strikes every one as the predominant characteristic, and a cheerful beaming of the eye that makes the countenance agreeable. You may see determination to do what he considers a duty; but you need never expect to see restless anxiety or fuss. He is the last being to whom we should have expected such terms to be applied as "fanfaronade," etc. Nichols certainly made a mistake here, and had his friend Kilpatrick in his mind when he drew that picture.[19] He must have recollected the appearance of that officer as Bombastes Furioso, challenging Wheeler out to fight, and imagined that he saw "le petit General," with a flag in his hand, calling over to Wheeler's men, in stentorian voice, "come out now, you set of cowardly skunks; you claim that you whip Kilpatrick every time, come out now and try it; and I'll not leave enough of you to thrash a corporal's guard. I am *Kill himself*." We almost looked for the boots and the well-known distich and supposed they might have been hung up, if they had not been lost in some of his hurried movements; such as occurred when surprised by Hampton, and in *dishabille*, he ran for the woods, leaving his mulatto doxy to follow as she could. There are several other remarks of Nichols' that ought to be noticed. Several soldiers were found on the road-side, who had been killed, either by the citizens or by Confederate soldiers. They belonged to a gang who had been firing and pillaging the country in every direction, and simply met the fate they deserved. The virtuous indignation of the General is aroused and Sherman gave Kilpatrick orders to hang and shoot prisoners who fall

---

19 Major General Hugh Judson Kilpatrick (1836-1881), whose nickname was "Kill-Cavalry," was Sherman's chief of cavalry.

into his hands, to any extent he considers necessary. Nichols' fire on the occasion, calls out: "Shame on Beauregard and Hampton and Butler," and asks, "Has the blood of their fathers become so corrupted, that the sons are cowardly assassins. If this murderous game is continued by their friends, they will bitterly rue the day it was begun." Without knowing why or wherefore those men were punished, an order is given for the hanging of the prisoners, though Sherman, when alluding to the circumstance, acknowledges that his foragers committed many acts of atrocity. To the question as to the corruption of the blood of the fathers leaving the sons assassins, I have only to say, if Nichols wishes an answer, he need only ask the question personally, and he can test the conditions of consanguinity. Men who have been employed in burning up the country, robbing the houses and turning out the families, to burn their dwellings, are to pass unmolested, because they wear the blue uniform of Sherman's thieves; but when a rebel soldier fires on one of their officers, although as he states, the poor wretch harmed no one, he was hanged at once for his attempted assassination; a fit commentary upon the statement made above.

A generous enemy would abstain from abusing his opponent, when no longer in the field. An officer of sense may, from want of tact, grandeurize himself and army, but would abstain from depreciating his antagonist. The pusillanimity of the foe necessarily detracts from the prowess of the conqueror, and he who would boast of a victory gained over decrepit old age or staggering infancy; would deem himself heroic in overcoming the coward and the driveller. For the army's sake, for his own share in the *glorious victory won by sixty-eight thousand men over fifteen thousand,* he should not sneer at the conquered, but to enhance his own merit, should make the Carolinians very paladins; the Cids of this century, who fought and defended every inch of their ground with the skill of Massena. Let me turn to one of the sentences in which he has vented his spleen and exhibited his folly. There are many of the same kind to be found in his work. "A characteristic of South Carolina chivalry has impressed itself upon all of us since we entered the State, and had a marked illustration last night and this morning, I refer to a whining, helpless, craven spirit, which shows itself whenever any of these people get hurt." "These fellows who were to die in the last ditch; who would welcome us with bloody hands to hospitable graves, are more cowardly than children, and whine like whipped school-boys. Ridiculously helpless, they sit and groan, without making an effort to help themselves." That statement is as false as ever was penned by a Yankee, and not a man, woman, or child six years old, but would pronounce the writer of such a paragraph, a miserable dastard, unused to the society of gentlemen, and incapable of appreciating what belongs to the class. The incident that he has mentioned of the Palmetto tree, ought to have made him blush, whilst he was writing such a slander. That tree was respected even by the rude soldier; and why? Because it recorded the names of the men who had been engaged in the Mexican war, and brought back with them a character surpassed by none other; because they knew that that Regiment saved the honor of the army, when the troops of New York and Pennsylvania driven back, exhibited their terror to the enemy. They could not advance on Chepultepec, but the Palmetto Regiment, though decimated in the previous fight, advanced against the enemy, supported the retreating forces of New York and Pennsylvania, allowed them to regain their *morale*, and enabled Scott to dictate his terms from the halls of Montezuma. Their sons and relatives have met the Yankees time after time in battle, and never given back one inch, with any thing of equal numbers. That they have not degenerated, let Bull Run, Seven Pines, Mechanicsville, Coal Harbor, and a host of other places testify. Not merely in those places, but you can scarce mention a battle which has been fought, in which the blood of the Carolina has not freely flowed. They beat you at Eton, the last battle in Carolina, when Butler drove back your forces. They fought you to the last.

Turn to the siege of Charleston—to Secessionville, and say whether any evidence of a craven spirit was there; or whether within the walls of Sumter, the whining of the whipped school-boy has been heard. The siege of that fort should have taught you to have used more truthful language. For more than a year, with your immense force, you tried to get possession of that one fortress and constantly failed. With your immense naval armament and land forces, you day by day, rained your iron balls and shells upon that devoted place, but she succumbed not; you beat down her walls, until she became a mass of ruins, yet still she defied you; and when her upper tiers were silenced and she could no longer return fire with her cannon, her note of defiance was still heard in the booming sound of the morning and evening gun. Twice you attempted to scale her battered walls, and twice she hurled your forces back, broken and discomfited; and yet you talk about the craven spirit of South Carolinian chivalry, as an object of the utmost disgust and contempt of the Northern officer and soldier. The expression was as false as it was anxiously desired to be, and in your heart you knew it to be a falsehood. You at last obtained the old fort; but how? Not by gallant conquest, but her own voluntary surrender. She could fight no more and the very flag which you have hoisted in triumph over her battlements, but reads you a lesson of disgrace. The stars and stripes that now flaunt over her battlements, tell you of a flag that had been struck after three days contest, and of others that were arrayed against it for over five hundred days, yet could never for a moment be planted on her soil. And the morning gun but recalls the recollection of that protracted struggle and the miserable failure. The assertion was false. No craven spirit was seen in the State; you heard no whining entreaties. They acknowledged themselves overpowered by your numbers, but not subdued by your bravery. They submitted to a necessity forced upon them, and made galling in the extreme by the *grossieries* of the victors. So far and no farther do they acknowledge. They still believe they were right, but like many others, similarly situated, they have yielded to the necessity of their position. They agreed to remain quiet, but they did not bargain for abuse from the ignorant and the vulgar. The force opposed to them was overwhelming, and their not being able to oppose, reflected neither disgrace nor dishonor. By Major Barry's account, Sherman had 68,000 effective muskets, besides cavalry, etc., and Nichols himself boasts that the footsteps of 100,000 abolitionists had pressed the sacred soil and broken down our spirits. To such a force was opposed the troops of Hardee, and the few men gathered together in a hurry and concentrated about Columbia—the aged and the boys; in all, not equal to the number that Sherman had in any one of his three Divisions, and 12,000 of these in Charleston, useless to the cause. Under such circumstances, they met and fought you and retarded your movements. To charge a people with cowardice for not beating back such hordes, could only have been made by a brutal mind, regardless of all the amenities of civilization. Let us see, if when he penned those lines, he believed in their truth. Had he forgotten his statement that "the rebels successfully defended their strong line of works on the north side of the Congaree creek, until about four o'clock this afternoon." "Our attempts to cross the river below, have met with earnest opposition." "I never saw more spirited determined fighting, than that of those few hundred brave fellows." If the fighting was spirited and determined on one side, it must have been equally so on the other, and whilst he has designated the number of those engaged on the one part, why not have said that their opponents were but a few men left to obstruct their march, whilst the rest of the army made good their retreat. Such expressions from any writer, throw doubt upon the narrative; but from an officer it reflects disgrace, and shows bitterness of mind that delights in traducing. Here let me stop; and I will only say, that I am yet to learn where, with equal numbers and a fair field, the Yankees ever got the better of the Southern Rebels.

APPENDIX

The following statements refer to the situation of military affairs, and the number of troops engaged on both sides, and have not been embodied in the foregoing account.

The disparity between the forces of the invaders and the defenders of the soil may be thus set forth. If the whole number of men under arms in South Carolina at the time of the entry of Gen. Sherman into the State could have been collected together they would have amounted to about 16,000. Of these, 12,000 were under Hardee, scattered along the coast; 2,600 were under Stephenson, collected chiefly from the fragments of the Western army; 1,400 under Wheeler, and 500 under Butler, or say, in round numbers 2,000 cavalry. With this small force it was attempted to hold in check Sherman's army of 75,000 men. Major Barry, the Federal Chief of Ordinance, in his report to Gen. Sherman writes: "The number of guns was reduced to one per thousand effective bayonets. The whole number of field batteries were sixteen, comprising sixty-eight guns, which were distributed as follows: 15th Army Corps, 18 guns; 17th Army Corps, 14 guns; 14th Army Corps, 16 guns; Cavalry, 4 guns. Total 68." Add to this force the officers, and the probability is that the army must have exceeded 75,000 men. Hardee soon withdrew to Charleston, and Sherman started through the swamps, on his grand tour to sever the railroads and reach Columbia. Nichols speaks of the want of spirit in defending the creeks, bridges, etc., which the Federals had to pass, and how they had turned our flank and dashed through woods and water to drive the enemy. He would lead the public to suppose that desperate assaults had been made against equal forces in which Yankee boldness and strategy had prevailed, when in fact our meagre numbers only enabled us to maintain a corps of observation, which was compelled to retreat whenever the enemy approached too near. In so doing our troops occupied calmly and in order, the next best position to which they were assigned.

If we had had 30,000 men the result, in all probability, would have been far different. Sherman would have been deprived of the pleasure of burning small villages, and indulging in the smaller game of stealing horses, killing cows, hogs, pigs, and sacking hen roosts and negro hovels. From the time Sherman passed Orangeburg there were opposed to him four thousand men, all told—a body which any one of his corps would outnumber by three to one. This small force constantly contested his advance; skirmished with him at Thom's Creek; obstructed his movements at Granby, and held him at bay. As Nichols acknowledges, "the rebels successfully defended their single line of works on the north side of the Congaree Creek until about four o'clock this afternoon," referring to the operations of the 15th, preceding their entry into Columbia. This was done by Wheeler, with about 600 men. Nichols continues: "Our attempts to cross the river below the city have met with earnest opposition. After sharp skirmishing we managed to get a few men across the river in boats. I never saw more spirited or determined fighting than that of these few hundred brave fellows," referring of course to the Federal advance guard. He pays further tribute to the gallantry of our little army in his account of the battle of Averysborough, when he writes, "The regiment of Charleston heavy artillery, made up of the best blood of Carolinas, was in our immediate front during the fight. It fought well, and suffered severely, both in officers and men. A larger proportion of officers were wounded in this fight than any fight I have known." Yet these are the men who had lost caste—had become so demoralized that it was impossible to recover their position, etc. He adds further, "The rebels have shown more pluck than we have seen in them since Atlanta." To be sure they were behind breastworks, and fully equaled us in numbers actually engaged; but they supposed the whole army would come up, which was half the battle to us in its moral effect upon them."

With such admissions as this, it is wilful slander and unworthy of any writer, who has the true feelings and principles of a gentleman, to make the statements we have just recorded.

To return, however, to the defence of Columbia. Sherman arrived here with the whole of his immense army confronted by not more than 5,000 men, all told; a difference of about twelve to one. This small force had been scattered over a space of thirty miles, and was in fact little more than an army of scouts. So if there by any disgrace attaching to the defence of the Capital of South Carolina, it surely rests on Sherman, who proved himself so dastardly in disposition, fiendish in temper, and brutal in conduct, as to devastate a country wholly incapable of protecting itself and completely in his power. Nor would he have attempted it, had Gen. Johnston been in command with a force of even 20,000 men. For that officer, with about that number of men, afterwards fought Sherman at Bentonville, and for three days held his great army, nearly three larger than our own, completely in check. Unfortunately, South Carolina could not have mustered 20,000 troops under any circumstances. Sherman knew the country was at his mercy and, like a fiend, he showed none. In his recent fourth of July speech, he boasts of having succeeded in effecting the results he intended, and virtually acknowledges the destruction he has so often denied. In fact, the great idol of the North, spoke scarcely a truth while in South Carolina. What confidence can be placed in a man who thus officially falsifies matters which come under his observation, and disparages an enemy whose prowess he had occasion to fear and to respect on every occasion.

We can only view the march of Sherman through Georgia and the Carolinas, as a Great Raid, conceived and carried out, simply because he anticipated no opposition. Hood's bold and unfortunate attempt in Tennessee left the door open. It was, in fact, safer for the Federal Commander to march to the coast than to retrace his steps. He came to Savannah because there were few or no obstacles in his way; he pressed forward to Columbia, because there were few troops in this direction to contest his advance, and he burnt the city to the ground, to gratify a fiendish spirit which revelled in the misery of his fellow men. If there is glory in this, let him and his friends make the most of it.

The impartial historian will record that in no single instance did Sherman ever whip Gen. Johnston, or Kilpatrick obtain the advantage of Gen. Hampton. In truth, Gen. Kilpatrick does not figure very boldly in the closing scenes of the war, with all the assistance of Nichols and Sherman. After his famous race to the swamp near Fayetteville, when he took his precipitate departure in his shirt and draws, leaving his fair and frail school marm behind, the great Yankee cavalryman kept well under the wing of the infantry.[20]

I close this brief review of the military operations of Gen. Sherman in South Carolina, with the following extract from a letter written by a distinguished officer, whose position enabled him to obtain correct information, and who moreover was a participant in the scenes to which he refers:

"At Congaree creek not more than 600 men of Wheeler's were engaged, and the enemy only succeeded in dislodging him by crossing the creek, above and below them. This fight held Sherman all day, and he camped that night near the Congaree creek. The infantry were withdrawn to the Columbia side of the river soon after dark and were followed by the cavalry. The bridge was burned contrary to orders. The order was for the Engineers to destroy one or two arches. Wheeler's command was placed, one brigade with Butler below Columbia, and the rest on the Saluda river. There were thus in Columbia, only 2600 infantry under Stephenson, Butler's cavalry, about 600 men, and one brigade of Wheeler's, about 400.[21] Wheeler fought at the Saluda, and between that and the Broad river, which he crossed on the evening of the 16th. At 8 A.M. on the 17th, Stephenson took Wheeler's place, and the latter marched higher up the river. There were about 4,500 to 5,000 men in all, guarding the river from Frost's plantation to Zeigler's Ferry, a distance of about 30 miles. The enemy crossed during the night of the 16th, in front of the infantry, and Gen. Hampton seeing that all defence was hopeless, ordered Stephenson to fall back. Soon after the sun rose on the 17th, Wheeler covered his withdrawal."

---

20 In March 1865, at Monroe's Crossroads, North Carolina, General Wade Hampton's cavalry made a surprise dawn attack on a camp of Union troops under the command of General Judson Kilpatrick, who fled the scene barefoot in his underclothes, leaving behind his lover, the beautiful Marie Boozer. She was the daughter of a Northern sympathizer who fled Columbia and took refuge with Kilpatrick, a notorious womanizer. During the Georgia campaign, he seduced and impregnated a Chinese girl named Molly who "had joined his entourage as a laundress." Martin, *Kill-Cavalry*, 208-09.

21 "Stephenson" was General Carter L. Stevenson (1817-1888).

An extract from Wheeler's report states that "about nine o'clock or half-past, when near the cross roads, two miles north of Columbia, I met the Mayor of Columbia in a carriage, preceded by a large white flag. I immediately ordered the firing to cease, and allowed him to pass on to the enemy. I withdrew up the Winnsboro road. Gen. Hampton shelled the camp of the enemy from the hills of East Granby on the night of the 15th, and Butler repelled quite a severe attack upon him. The artillery lost six or seven horses killed, and there were quite a number of men wounded.

"From Chester, we turned and got on both flanks of the enemy, and had almost daily skirmishes, some quite heavy. Every day from 50 to300 prisoners were brought in. The Provost Marshall reported upwards of 3,000 prisoners turned over by the cavalry, and think nearly as great a number were killed and wounded. About 100 wagons, 400 head of cattle and several hundred head of horses, were captured in the campaign. Sherman's whole loss from the time he left Columbia to the end of the struggle, was not less than 10,000 men. At Fayetteville, about 100 Yankee cavalry came in when our troops were there; eight men charged them, routed them, killing eight and capturing nine— the leader and seven men. Near Fayetteville, Kilpatrick was attacked and his camp was taken, with upwards of 500 Yankees and 173 of our men, who were prisoners. Kilpatrick escaped in his shirt and draws only, leaving his fair and frail Yankee school marm, in our hands. One of our boys assisted in dressing her and let her go to her protector. At Bentonville, Gen. Johnston attacked Sherman. Two corps drove him a mile, took three guns, and a line of breastworks. Had his whole force been in position he would have defeated Sherman entirely. With 18,000 men, he held his position in front of Sherman's whole force, strengthened by Schofield's corps for three days, and then retreated without loss. From _____ to Hillsboro, the cavalry were engaged every day, covering the retreat of the infantry. Some of these affairs were quite serious, and all creditable to our army. The day before Raleigh was evacuated, it was desirable to check the advance of the enemy as much as possible, in order to remove the stores, etc. With one brigade only, and Butler's Command, and two batteries of artillery, two corps of the enemy were so steadily engaged, that they advanced only five miles in six hours. When we evacuated Raleigh,

Kilpatrick charged Hampton's rear-guard. We turned on him, charged and drove him back in confusion, taking prisoners, and killing and wounding some of his men. This was the last fight of Hampton's command and it was a success."

Now let me ask with such facts before him, Nichols being Sherman's aid, what epithet should be attached to his *honored name*, when he could pen the following lines.

"The Rebels hope that Johnston will be able to recall and reinforce that army; but no man living has that power. He might as well try to reclothe the naked limbs of those oak trees yonder on the hill side, with last years foilage of green; or a task more impossible yet, restore to the Southern Gentleman, their lost reputation for chivalry, honor and manhood."

BIBLIOGRAPHY

PUBLISHED PRIMARY AND SECONDARY SOURCES

Chesnut, Mary Boykin. *A Diary from Dixie*. Ed. Ben Ames Williams. Cambridge, MA.: Harvard University Press, 1980.

Cisco, Walter Brian. *Wade Hampton: Confederate Warrior, Conservative Statesman*. Washington, D.C.: Potomac Books, 2004.

Huger, Alfred. "The Burning of Columbia: Letter from Hon. Alfred Huger." *New York World,* August 22, 1866.

Keys, Thomas Bland. *The Uncivil War: Union Army and Navy Excesses in the Official Records*. Biloxi, Miss.: The Beauvoir Press, 1991.

Martin, Samuel J. *Kill-Cavalry: The Life of Union General Hugh Judson Kilpatrick*. Mechanicsburg, PA: Stackpole Books, 2000.

Stokes, Karen. *South Carolina Civilians in Sherman's Path*. Charleston, SC: The History Press, 2012.

Trezevant, John Timothee. *The Trezevant Family in the United States*. Columbia, SC: The State Co., 1914.

MANUSCRIPTS

South Caroliniana Library, University of South Carolina:

Daniel H. Trezevant. Manuscript Volume, 1865.

Grace Brown Elmore Diary, 1860-1866.

South Carolina Historical Society, Charleston, SC:

Lee, Eliza Lucilla Haskell. "Reminiscences of Troublous Times, and God's Special Providences." Unpublished manuscript, 1884.

Library of Congress, Manuscripts Division:

McCarter Journal, 1860-1866.

Latest Releases & Best Sellers

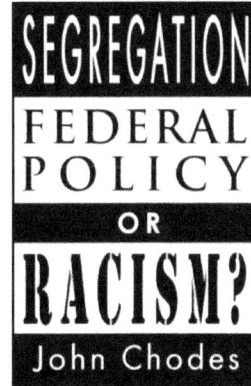

OVER 70 UNAPOLOGETICALLY SOUTHERN
TITLES FOR YOU TO ENJOY

SHOTWELLPUBLISHING.COM